Ornate With Smoke

Ornate With Smoke

Sterling Plumpp

Third World Press
Chicago

01 00 99 98 97 5 4 3 2 1

Acknowledgment. Thanks to the editors of TriQuarterly where two sections from *Ornate With Smoke* appear.

Cover design by Taahira Mumford

Library of Congress Cataloging-in-Publication Data

Plumpp, Sterling, 1940-
      Ornate with smoke /Sterling Plumpp
         p. cm.
    ISBN 0-88378-193-X (cloth).
    ISBN 0-88378-198-0 (paper).
    1. Blues (Music)—Poetry. 2. Jazz—Poetry. 3. Afro-American—Music—Poetry. I. Title.
    PS3566. L79076   1997
    811'.54—DC21
                             97-22954
                                 CIP

Third World Press
7822 S. Dobson
Chicago, IL 60619

Dedication

For Fred Anderson:
Improvisor

Table of Contents

Preface

❧❦

    For a very long time in my existence on this planet on this side of the Atlantic, I had no idea of why I breathe. But the last forty-two years of my life have indelibly defined my mission here. I should have known that cold wet Saturday in 1955 when they transported what remained of my grandfather across the highway in angled masonic salutes that, somehow, I was here to dialogue with slaves. For a six-foot deep hole saturated with antebellum bones of my ancestors drew him into the earth. I should have known when my daddy, C.H., black as any kente lineage, went back near "Ernest Robinson's Quarters" to reside beneath ground adjacent to St. Paul's Church. I should have known in 1980 when my mother, Mary (Scootie)—the first of my grandparent's children to die—led me in a cortege to near where my grandparents' parents had been in bondage. I should have known in August of 1982 when my uncle, Walter, succumbed to cancer and had a battle command of jimpson weeds giving pungent salutes to his name on land where chains once held his forebears hostage. I should have known in 1990 when my aunt, Carrie, was placed in a vault less than two miles from where she and her parents before had been born to till land they could never own. And finally, in 1993, when my grandmother, Mattie Emmanuel—Momma—closed her eyes as a goodbye, I knew that I was put here to work in the field hollers of my people.

    I view the journey from some savannah in West Africa, be it home of Mandinka, Wolof, Ashanti, Fanti, Ewe, Yoruba, Ibo, or Ibibio—across the nightmarish horrors of the middle passage, and finally to changed names and bondage on these shores as a series of processes I invent and reinvent every day I live. I perceive my ancestors invented and reinvented many languages in order to spread literacy among embattled souls: Negro Spirituals, Folktales, Sermons, Blues, Jazz, Gospel, Soul, Do-wop, and Rap. As a poet, I see these linguistic inventions as launching pads where my imagination is free to search eternity for an appropriate language for me to get through another day. I have no past, no present, and no future unless I invent language to evoke it.

Blues and jazz differ for the poet in this respect. Though in both, one has to locate one's individuality and improvise nuances to suit one's personal tongue. The invented language of blues empowers the poet to speak his name and his journeying through naming pains while the invented language of jazz allows the poet to acquire a map of the territory of imaginations that changes and expands. Jazz as poetry constantly begs improvisation, re-definitions in terms of moods and rhythms—demands perpetual journeys into cells of self by a selfless self.

Ornate With Smoke is my way of saying to jazz and its inventors that I am jazz and my soul breathes its riffs in order to survive to invent another day. It is my way of saying thanks to the music which brings literacy to the spirit.

Sterling D. Plumpp

Ornate With Smoke

I. LAW GIVER IN THE WILDERNESS

Coltrane
takes the night
train to Small's Paradise
Lost in urban
renewal landscapes

From Von I learn Be
Bop is the under
ground language of the spirit
and you play where some
body picks in a wind
ukelele quartet: baby don't you
wanna go back to that same old place

sweet home Chicago

And I
visit you in the Bird
House in tornadic
corridors of wind
but not before I
find you up
where you sit in the pent
house of the grand upper
room and I get Mahalia

to take me there in octaves of
her Gospel Commuter of Hallelujahs
Prez and Coleman and Jug all
ways take down in the basement
on silences between night

trains and Coltranes just
before the break of day
light years where I am Ewart
bound and hire a dirigible
and a five-year-old Didgeridoo-rag
time for my voice

You are a be
bopper popping the shoe
shine rag in ear
phones of tomorrows where twelve
Gabriels audition in Bowie's
triumphs in night
shadows of special futures
he riffs just for a
thrill and Satchmo's trumpet
wrapped in green onions

From Von
I learn the saxophone
is a tenor law
giver in the wilderness of
loneliness where he presides
over ballads dueling the sun
shine for bragging rights
in the torrid sky
lines of Chi
town chitlin switch
boards where all the hear
say is one big party
line

He
takes twelve bar
bells of blues
and fans his
self-proposed adventures in
to theories
of physical touches and gate
ways he inscribes on platinum
nodes of his fingers

adjusting moods to his scotch
or cognac or vodka or bourbon memories
misty in B-flat
lands where Jesse James
mows his lawn and Billy the kid
napped laughter of his wife in
laws jumps from glass
house to glass
house
to house parties
even in the New Apartment

From Von
I learn

II. Ornate With Smoke

Remaking:
a distinguished breakage.

The
fountain of language
discoursing with every
day feet. In postures of
wings. Stem of a tongue
rising from debris of a
Trane ornate with smoke.

Short
bursts of air signify. A century of
silence recoiled
in tenor moments you
revive. Velvet totems of faces
you wear. Ricocheted touches.
Jamming with masks of iron
and thunder tap
dancing with rattling
feats of rhythms.

You
have been here
before.

And I

know you from hemorrhages of light
years. I hear Miles
down hives of the Be
bopping itch to create.

Avalanches I prepare.
Atoms I raise.
Clouds I mime.
Montages of demons I translate.

I pursue languages of my foot
step children of swing in Dixie
land or at Minton's.

Dissonance
is a ventriloquist calling
my speech from dry bones
through silent drums. Down to McCall's
voice.

Is the do
rag common
denominator of riffing paths
through nights of bone mountains.

I chew terrible bubble gum
bo arrows of speech.
I order from Mingus's catalogs
of tonight at noon
or Ornette's tomorrow.
Tonight is
the night I be
head youth.

Cryptic dialogues of alien
greetings in chords are slaps on my back
water blues. I drink muddy
logic sleep in cold
train's box
cars of innovative ceilings. I adjust.

I do
not need to sign an agreement of
unity with a foreign
language. In order to speak my mother
tongue.

I
come from death and after
thoughts. Of another life on chromatic planes of
How I Got Over and No Hiding Place and Strange
Fruits. I pick from vine
yards of Birds and Counts and Dukes and Poppa
Got Brand New Bags of maps.
I file in my imagination.

I
find staples of my diet in hors d'oeuvres.
On kaleidoscopic menus of chance
and my axe leases an apartment
from tenements of pain
and begin teaching sultry
liaisons with a geography.
Circumscribed by holy
rollers and the mighty rock
church inventions of shouts.
In the face of bleeding ulcers of
forecasts of rain on my days.

A generation robbed.
Of its cacophony
is illiterate.

I got black cat
a combs in dread
locks of the Rubic
on off nights I back
stroke to back
beats of Handy melodies
I feel and shout:

Yo
rub a belly of dialects
I name with windows I
open with riffs of a good
morning glory
I offer

Nommo auction clocks
for me
Nommo auction clocks
for me
Nommo auction clocks
for me

I watch my shadow perform
at rodeo stations of the cross
my dreams rise from membranes of
thieves to sing

Nommo auction clocks
for me

I am an old seventy-eight
My forty-fives are empty
The thirty-third and
one third degree of
my father's masonry
spins meandering in unemployment
lines

Nommo
Nommo
Nommo

I am responsible for language
I live
in The A Cappella Dew
Drop Inn
where I hear years of silences
shift into drive

As Malachi, the Calysonian of Rhythms,
pastes his colors betwixt
between pulses of blood
on the corner of jive and Mister Down
Child

The Judge
gives me ninety-nine
years on Parchment Farm
and I harvest signatures of dust
jackets I wear

I wake
in little E
we we hours of screaming

Give me
a glass of Rum
boogie at Basin
Street car salvage
missions

I am locked out
done lost McKie's

Throw me
out my juke boxer
shorts so I can improvise
this ring

By
the dawn's early Light
Henry Huffing and puffing
to heal
some brother inflicted
by white
rejection but exhibiting
symptoms of cancer

9

I wear
a Crown
Propeller on my little finger
for good lucky
strikes down lanes of white
approval but I fail

I find VeeJay data
bases in the Regal voices do
woping and motowning high
ways I travel
till the Sun
Ra boats of oarsmen
orchestrate paradigms of high
hat blues talking trash
in broken accents of salutations
in other galaxies

where I staff light
years for the good
times

I am just Da
homey a long ways
from my home
land
lords

I build settlement
hospices for old days

Yo
rub a dialect
I bring from sounds I heave
Yo
rub a language I sling
between rocks I use
as pillows

I am just Da
homey a long ways
from home
I am just Da
homey a long ways
from home

Strike
a match to hear my sound
Strike
a match to hear my sound

I am broke and alone
I am always prism bound

III. Indigo Street

My
soul was torn
and my pa
pa loi did
not feel I could
riff it on my own
so he got Henry
to Thread
Gill my wound
with sonic needles
that give immaculate eye
sight to a Venetian
blind standing on a corner

He
breaks off the head
start program of a distant planetary
moon and blows down
home blues from its neck
tie with gurgling cadences of
Roscoe getting his little
bit of tenor appellations in down
beat troughs of Ayler

And you
there all the while
speaking
in different lineages of
dreams   I know

I long

When I long
I hear

You
paraphrase eternity in colors of the rain
forest   Near trombone
boulevards of lazy shadow
boxing lyrics of ballots
cast for body and
soul of a man's
world of Poppa with a good
foot passed to the high
ways you design in mind
routes for Jasper Jones and
Shine

I hear

Europe intrepid in war
robes of laughter you rinse
from Roman night in
gales you breathe

through ruins of Caesar
salads for a melody

I feed
fifty thousand demons
in my pen
name with indigo street
cars of desire For
A Trains on Harlem's rail
road maps of Semple's
feet Where Langston
drinks laughter spilled
from a saxophone pitcher of
genius   I hear in velvet
orchards calling
your name

And
Europe crawls from a cocoon of
silences between your riffs
to sing

IV. GRIS GRIS AND MOONSHINE

You got yourself a Ham
Id with
out a super
ego on the road of
criminality like St Paul
Drake who collects evidence
for Mason/Dixie
land coronets on trial
accused of blues with a feeling
but your axe acquits
with the holy writ
ten mountains of truths
in your closed eyes
where justice resides in bass
mint juleps of your solos

And you wear cape cod
liver oil wells of odors

Shout
into the field
larks sailing like the King
Bee buzzing round
your baby's door
where your win
dow jones average is ten
thousand

Each
night you lay down in sleepy hollow
logs crying I
        for
        got
        ten miles of myths with my seven
steps to heaven

Do
the huckle
buck and wing
dang doodle on canvasses of
my dreams

Because I ride the El
Zu Bar
tending thunder special
delivery of gris
gris moon
shine

I set the table
cloth of montages
where my soul dines

Got
my own cross
bow slinging arrows of speech
therapy

From Von
I learn extended solos in
to voyages in
side a self
less self   Music ain't no
thing but history in a short
hand of improvisation

Voice
of generations talking trash
cans for lies

Voice
out of the voices
of silent choruses

Speaking
dialects of tenor voyages in
to saxophone glossaries
the length of a decade
in a minute

Where I do
the huckle
buck and wing
dang doodle sketches
of Maxwell street
carnivals of black
night falling

Von
takes a rhythm on leave
from swing
promotes it to be
bopping chordal light
leap years he choreographs
from tones of Boni Maroni
and the bad man Stagger
Lee switch
blading tracks of my tears

Where
you are all
ways the rumpus
room mate of Sutherland
breezes spilling apple
cider on Magnolia tree
top hats of caricatures of
spirits burned at stakes of in
human kindness

In your versions of
what
is this thing called
love me with a feeling

V. Unstaked Silences: Lessons from a Master

Von
is a master surge
on stormy clouds
eyes
He for
sakes scalpel and laser
for the razor he knows
so well. His riffs
got the first lessons in sharpness
and wit from them.

He
assists you in voyages in
side skin in search of spiritual
ailments. But I just can
not find him in no white
jacket. Or taking no hypocritical
oath. I am no geneticist, though
I know Von is in your laboratory of grimaces
and you are
in his walks in
to light
years each time he ventures from Birds
and Monks and Miles of inventions. Some
body told me
Von was commissioned for back
ground music for stars marching to stations
in the universe's orchards of light. Said you
are a planet man
din
go in
side a river's voice naming and naming.

I hear
you called tailor be
cause war
robes for stars in your soloing journeys
cross every bit of silence. Said you got tenor
maps of all unstaked silences in your riffs.

Every
night I grow mute
I sleep on jazz's floor.

Your
music, its tentacles of excavation,
reaching towards the navel of memory,

Welcomes
the slave
ships after centuries

it opens its arms to them for citizen
ships they board to humanity
your music
is both door
and door
way to gates of tomorrows
through yesterdays' labyrinths of
nadirs and horizons of breathing air
ships you invent

tenor meat
loaves of the feeling
you had last night
time is the right
time be in loops of journeys
you name and name

VI. MANNA

Like
getting a long over
due letter from God by
way of Mars and several galactic river
bed settlements of light

Your
song reveals covenants renewed with self
determination to ride dreams and I all
ways find my self a
lone note in the bottom of a looking
glass of milk when I hear you in

side the menagerie where I split
my soul and feed half light and
the other half dark melons of your rhythms with
out seeds or grand table
manners

This
is a tale be
tween breaths I take
an interloper of tongues
between inhale
and exhale testing
sites of creation and
silences I invest portfolios of tears
I wring patterns of sound
and color and touch

This
is my story in the innocence of
its open palms

and its fingers' will to climb
logos of breathing
I sing because migratory blue
birds of tenor axes perch
on the shadow of plantations
clouding my vision with indigo memories of cotton
mouth words that strike my dreams

sing tall trees dreams
ascend to find three hundred
pounds of heavenly joy and St.
James Infirmary/Lord for the hard
times/Yeah for the hard
times

You
and Von bleed for fibers of
ballads lyrical evocations
for testimonies of feelings
tilling in swamps you hack
with tones and turnings in
side out up
side some devil's head
gear shifted in
to improvised lengthy solos
probe depths with riffs of rib
tip mornings in Negrille garbs of
holy Ja
pan
cakes with omelettes mixed
with gris gris syrup McCoy pours
over Trane
cakes while Llyod sets the temperature
for cooking and Elvin just sits
and orders his choice from thunder

Each
riff you command to battle ship
mates of Ornette is a new reality
I index with blue markers
on detailed maps of my spirit
where I survey journeys I plan

Each
nine
teen year old
that got ways just like a baby
child that journeys
from your solos and rises from a stray
horn give me the lush
life I reach for on pages

That
got no hiding
place in the deep
river of your voice
where all God's chilluns
got a home and where Von riffs
riffs so sweet/I hear the tambourines
of angels' feet

VII. SEVEN

I do
ordinary chores of a motown
house boy who sells salt
peanut buttered calls and responses
to his shadow arrested at Bloomingdale's
for trying on equality

From Billie's Bounce
I buy Sarah a new hand bag
lady but Sweeney Todd is still
convicted for stabbing customers behind wall
green's counters where he establishes Contact
lens for his dementia

My daddy
was born in a run
down mono
log
cabin where his boot
legs of stills

March
with white lightning
bugs for sorghum home
steads of light
bread and butter
beans

I am straight
jackets of selves beat
into regiments for voice
mail at Fannie Mae's
Cafe where the blues is all
right in Milton's casserole of
murders on his hands

Negotiating
for spoils of destruction
I prevail with lyrical
antidotes of flues
I investigate

I am the steeple
jack of all trades
between heaven and rising
sons of gun
slingers who rescue ballads
from Dillinger and Capone
and James
town an illegitimate dream gunned down
town on Satyr
nights

On the spot
where gestures are play
grounds dis
interred so yesterdays
can achieve equal
opportunity of expressions
in your facial translations of
Nile related moans
you purchase from country
road-arrested fingers

Jails are concrete
catacombs with
out bones of saints except for Saint
Nicholas sentenced
for his sleigh of stolen good
times in blood red sacks
of dreams

The amendment of laughter
is ratified
by majority voting
rights of air-filled
jaws in search of prey

Blues
is just the dis
co-chair of my imagination

Calls
meetings to order
scrambled egg
heads

VIII. Axe Journey

Where
I take excursions on my axe
I
dive into my solos as bass
but come up
drum for tenor pianissimo
of Bird's alto laughter
and Bechet's soprano supplications
humming above orbiting hatreds

I
chase some
thing like do-wop corners
where Jerry and Curtis
lead exoduses of genius
out of projects into
recorded revelations
where I locate umbilical journeys
of history tied onto to
morrows I distill riffs
from compact coffins my children
ride from infancy to premature
holes in the ground
there is this rare property
of signifying brooks and green
fields in my madness

Here
I sing "yesterday" and chorales
of broken hearted winds swing
low in my mother's faint
memory grows for Christmas

Here I cast a
nets for puzzles of foot
steps in windows of wind
and sand and rain

I
must fear my cross
examinations of clouds
I record
fifty-five years a
go in directions of wayward tales

Because the Big
Boss Man recorder of my story
was found
floating in the Chicago
river drown from over
dosages of self
importance

My songs
are just spirituals
with their skull
caps on backwards

IX. Unremembered

Beneath
years gone by
beneath ground
beneath graves

is myth
possessing drum soldiers

I hire
because naming pains

is an assault
on hours
seizing my voice

I need short night
times and long right
times I am in love with
out pensions for yesterdays
that worked for my songs
on the nightly county
farms I high
jacked with lyrics

My
daddy give me
a piece of rope his daddy
say he find it near Money Can't
Save You Mississippi/up
the pass from Money where Emmett
Till was killed

Ropes lying
on a carpet of dust
moaning narratives of its journey
through this world

I
was just a little rope
happy to be holding logs
on wagons or tying down
tarpaulin on trucks or
keeping some shoat or
yearling from kicking or
running away

Till
I got lost and the lynchers
find me they
call me Plaited Fear
say the best way to show
a nigger how not to act
give him a special fashion
show where all he wears
is a rope

My first model
was twenty and jet
black and struck over
seer for slapping his Momma
cause she did not know
the way to his bed

I remember
his wails like a drunken saxophone
blaring against choirs of
insects intoning darkness and silence
I remember his history shaking me
when they set fire
to his feet
on till he
is still
born again in my fibers
where I can
not stand the smell of sorrows

I know
many models
all with flames reaching
through skin for spirits
in rebellion
I know
many models
all black boys and
black men
They
stay some
where-abouts in
side space I carve
from my masters'
orders

When
your daddy tell you
he gon play rope
he saying he gon
play unremembered
memory your tenor voyages
speak in seven
teen dialects of Be
language it
self on trials
and errands for imagination

X. Riff Between Silence

I am a photograph of death
and my world
is a gallery   Each riff
between silences is
an opening

He
attends with his alligator
tales and pitch
black moods of harvests

Louis
thinks jams are familiar
reunions of sound
checks in heaven or hell
hounds congregating
at Twelve Bars of Invention
where a washer woman
cleans white folks,
floors and patches,
she picks up to make
quilts

I collect
patterns stitched fragments
of memory of dry bones
But I
release them only to have
my axe chop off a head
line on the wind in minor
leagues where Jackie refines
submission of curses in his voice
less shouts of invisibility
But he does not   I repeat
he does not play
in novels

I was drafted in
to The Navel of song on Decoration
Day after John Lee rows
his little boat across
ruins of the Titanic that
sinks in his tears

and Monk hears confessions
with laughter and signifying cutting
the rug montages of shadows
he uses as side mentors
for his chords

I explain it all But
don't hush   Like Billie
I arrange mutinies in nuances
and sign treaties
with agonized naming nameless
pains and loneliness in voices
of my axe where I play hide
and-go-seek new worlds some
how

Every day
Every day
Every day

I reed newspapers
for improvisation's sake
on some ministerioso street
I beam with sun
shine on a rainy day

Since I fell for you
round bout midnight
when a smokey leaf
taps on my windows'
pains   I call
my axe's voices
from nights in Tunisia
and wakeful bossa nova
cain inns

where dream creates a space
for spiritual jumbalayas to race
and I keep
Basie and Mingus on deck

Of that Old Ship made
of papier-mache golf
courses where Newk swings over
bridges of river choirs

Night is a comic strip
dancer I bribe
for hints about indigo
dice rolling seven
or eleven Miles
again and again

Funny How some dudes
can run miles
but can't take a single
original step across
the bridge

From Von
I learn an ash
tray is an oasis
if
your caravan of soundings
in pauses can read a desert's
naps

If
your world is a side street
car Duke drives up
town and down
harem rivers
where he hides jokes

XI. Language at Midnight

I am a defense attorney
in overcrowded jumbalaya
courts of a moan's grief
I defend style

My
screams are hallucinatory note
books I issue
my language at midnight

I place want ad
libs on barrels of sorrows
because when I play in dark
shade corridors of memory
I use baby funnel
clouds to wipe spider
traps from sounds
that swirl and twirl and spin
hopping reggae estates of Jah
over ska mountains and rock
steady plains and calypso hills down
home blues in damaged
control registers of Jacquet
blowing Canadian sun
sets over Niger falls

where I
con breaks between my tales in
to acreages of bottom
land
lords who lease me miles

I pursue my journey
Git on board odysseys of Prez
who chastises lightning
with his putting on dogs
of ballads riffing finger
prints of wet
nightingales

I am elected King
Biscuit Valedictorian in saw
dust nights Sonny
Squeezes blues
in the night when he flags down a Cab

Worry
Worry
Worry

All
I can do rag
time or swing or be
bop distance at sock
hops or rock and
roll attempts of taking
my name away
on their vacancy channels of
authenticity

I all
ways got one more mile
one more mile
to go counting my troubles

All
I can do is rap
black, beige and
brown stone cold
feelings on tenements of
wind where I some
times find Buddy crying
in his dark
room mates of squeezing with Christian
or Burrell developing incense
visions for troubles
just from the cotton
field
hollers walking back
streets

At least
God give Noah an Ark
to ride waves of the flood
and I got a axe to hack
my way from depths
to heights and from
widths to widths
I blow to keep
from going down
down
down where my nose
is in the sand

I blow
to keep from drowning
in water or
on dry land

XII. Dreams Without Interruption

There are
so many miles down in
side my triumphs
with backs towards
the audience
that I can
not possibly answer the phone

when some
racist bull
dozer rings in my dreams

I long
a place where I can
play
my dreams with
out interruptions
and listen
to their silent echoes
repeating my mother's
deifying whispers in
inner ears of the song
I long   And set
out to wind round
my journeys

My music is sustaining
speech working over
titles half a Sabbath
I borrow   from Ornette
corn pone months   Jug
rents for mashed potatoes
and Jimmy Smith's home
cookin' organ grinding index
cards for names of journeys
within the journey of one
solo out to lunch with Dolphy
on bass clarinet voyages
into nights Bechet barters
for

My music is arm
length of welcome for cold
rainy hats I wear at Harold's chicken
neck bones piled in City
Hall among the twenty
nine kings without thrones
who claim his crown
royale where bad
tastes   are dumplings for sugar
on the corner of sixty
third and cottage cheese
heads screaming how I
got over my soul looks back
and wonders how I got
over

XIII. ONLY THING I KNOW

I want

to get to a sub
division of heaven

And Dizzy
says he sells Bird
wings and salt
peanuts and wild Irish
girls popping fingers
to Bags at any Be
bop shop be
bopping clouds side
their heads for
bidding windows
for axes in view of landscapes

where life is a
wrinkled canvass I straighten
blow my names over chromatic
colors dodging light

with a one-eyed angel
child crying gardenias
of misty blue silences
pulling head down home
land in mercy lyrics
from burned tree
trunks of goodness America
sells black skins

I tip
toe on Dexter's twelve
bar shoulders toting battle
epics of breaks between lineages of
chords he commissions for journeys
into space ship
yards where Bird holds
seances

Only thing I know is a world
endless and inner in its voices
galactically mapping boulevards
for dreams for journeys
for sojourns for all
the worlds I know worlds I renew
my subscriptions to out of missions
into selves I discover inside my
self and self
less steps I venture

Each riff
is an epistle
I address to silhouettes
of screams some
times my solos are apostles
extolling white
elephants at phamous lounges
where Zambezi and Nile
shed tears and wash the face of time

I play
what's in front of me
And I
give all my songs poly
gram test sites
as wedding gifts

Biblical
lines of epiphany
I get from scratching
in innovative riffs
where I work five
laundry years
for my ballads

From Von
I learn I have
to get an injunction
get my syllabus
out pawn as I visit enterprize
zones of the spirit in his Von
ski masks telling jokes
to the Hawk in summer
time I learn New
Apartmentology in one
semester of a solo get
my Riff Certificate of Moods

I am
a geography of musicians
battle axes in cases
crying holy holy
rollers in my songs

where Americanization
is a rite of passage
with a failed grade
A racism

XIV. DEFINITION OF GOOD

Ornette
says I am the only person in the milky
way who kills
with a cross bow
tie

My
roving solos
get affirmative
reaction blues when some noble blue
I take his place
side a t-bone with
out a spoon
full of the good stuffing
in a baked cornish joke
or side a Trane on mid
galactic marathons between
his breath and fingers
tipping their hats to miles and
miles of funny valentines

Or side Eric out to lunch
with dolphins on violins of
sonar waves or side Cannon
ball rolling gazes of Big Joe
Turner shaking his make
shift worlds into gears of Louis
Jordan and Caldonia

Or side the mighty B.B.
gunshots of the Bad
Axe cutting some wood
stock or any
thing solid rock
or rolling stone
cold feeling in Buddy's
labyrinths inside his fingers'
voices shouting their right to vote or
to the tree of life
boats hitched in cries of country folk
medicines of songs
and dances

Way
out on the out
skirts of blue
notations at the Village
moving Tauhid into
midget captions on worn five dollar bill
boards or subdued under clankings of
a glass a damsel without mental dress

hums some
where over blues funded foot
pats

Or side store
front riffs from tongues
batting lyrics to clapping hand
jive interiors of scats of souls on ice
bergs in the promised
lands Ella scats to Sarah
who scats to Betty
who swallows the milky
way lodged challenges and

spits out humpty dumpty long
ago notes for Bird and
Diz to erect duplex montages
in nuances of the sky
lined up for their gigs

Moby Dick
Tracy is a friend of mine
He
makes waves when he searches for green
dolphin street or drinking
gourd lane

I find out
Stitt is really a rat
race car driver in grooves of Holmes
in the moon
glow of some
body's back
door

And I
learn time
breaks of my poems sing a
long roads with a saxophone
running long
distance prayers for them
selves and dreams
They speak

easy in other time
zones of mood
indigo baccalaureates of journeys
the axe man travels

Before drum calls
encores to memory

I hold
the record shop
lifting dreams
from universal
joints in my songs

Ain't no
body's business
card but my own night
time

Where
I got a bad axe handle
with care packages for the good
time clocks I breathe in
and out
side walks of life
times I unravel in upper
rooms of silences

I am sick
and sick and tired of
losing and I roll my ball
ads on Saturday supplements
nobody knows
the troubles I see see writer

because folks whisper
I am an amateur
and I am pro
choice

a recorder
in a love supreme
courts of hoops

Give me
one shot
gun house of bourbon on the rock
of ages with a glass of water
falls on the side
shows I swim just for thrill
gone for a while
every body in Chitown
is on a Dyett

Lose
weight
                    and can riff faster
faster

XV. Fifteen

Blow man
Blow

Each note
I meditate
is a crafted len

Each chord
I pray
is a new heart
beat

Each riff
I commission
is a dimension
of hours

And
every solo
I breathe
is a day

Blow man
Blow

They
crack
up a road
for a meal

Bird wants some
thing scrambled
Diz longs some
thing baked

This
is breath
This invention

Blow man
Blow

When stars grow
dim I can
not call Jug

he might jam
things up worse
or pour on
gasoline or put
dynamite on them

But
Prez blow sweet
fire into embers

And
Mingus refuels star
ships out of
gumption and Saturday
night beats up tempo up

side Shango's head
lines clapping hinges
to swing open Ogun's
Dogon postures

Blow man
Blow

Birds wants
Diz longs

This breath
This invention and
invention

Blow man
Blow

Muhal
peddles rogue
maps of imagination
from the cold
cuttings on bad
avenue and mornings
he bandages with
keys

Blow man
Blow

Joseph puts out wild
firing squads of self
hatred and screams

to Ornette
and Albert
and Eric

I am a text
less ranger now

Blow man
Blow

In
this world of
hind pockets

Two Tranes comin

One alto with a Jug
in its hands
The other tenor moments
in my baby's arms

A griot in long
johns hollers
from a vacant second
floor kitchenette

Hey,
Daddy-yo

What that over there
What you doin here
Hey, Daddy-yo
Look at the moon cryin
over there What the sun
doin lyin here

Blow   man
Blow

I
born to dye hours
I
born to wet
clouds
I
born to squeeze dry
land from weeping winds

I'm gonna move
just gotta move
way out on the out
skirts of sound

I'm gonna move
always gotta move
way out on the out
skirts of sound

I play
up a laser river
I play
up a laser river

I name
my pains get
them birth
certificates

I play
up a laser river

A urban star
hound prowling
for arts of eloquence
and inventions

Blow man
Blow

XVI. SIXTEEN

Worlds collide inside my axe
each time
I solo

I learn to speak
tenor on the page

I learn
other saxophone languages
even those from under foot
notes of Tranes
I did
not yet ride

So I
come to you asking
if I can be a bird
house boy bumming
rides from your solos in
to kitchen
pots and pans some
body's great grand
mother played when her sweet
daddy done
done her wrong

Bumming
rides into yesterday
with two or three stops in tomorrow
or bumming through midnights today
with two or three stops into day
breaks a thousand years ago

Can I be a bird
house boy with a pen
to blow his years clear of
the leaves memory sheds in autumn

I play
cynanide rhythms
for hurricanes

I do
rag
I do
rag
I do
rag on lies
I do
rag
I do
rag
I do
rag time

Because I
con breaks

I
con breaks
I
con breaks
I
con breaks

and
I do
rag
I do
rag
I do
rag time

XVII. Seventeen

King
marches to get the right
to vote but Satchmo
laughs to get the right
to voice and Bird takes flight
to get the right
to voyage where

Trane is a milky way precinct
captain registering soloistic
exploits on tenor axes but Dizzy

sails around the Cape of King
cotton mouth debts to give
floggings with his loggings of what salt
pork endeavors done done for brown
eyes and crowder peas

Out of the parenthesis of sleep
I lease a dog
on bad axe that cries militancy
boxing air with double
bladed jabs into facades of
deliverance

Tears running down
my face represent a museum of ruins
I find in cries along 43rd and the Big
Dipper filled with way out
troubles   where each riff
I breathe is a tour
guide for dreamers who long
geographies of silence

But Bird rises against kitchenette
skies to say no
body will ever pave
crazy streets in imagination

And Dizzy
replies no
body will ever name them
either

But I
ain't yet convinced
and got some knick
knacks for them

Did
the devil ever
record on Chess
Records with lynch
roped neck
bones or blue
notary publics of ships
docked in my mother's tears
or on VeeJay
birds collecting grains of sand
for files of evil going
on inside a harmonica's
voice or on bad
axe monuments Fridays
when the eagle flies
its kite in my dreams

Or did he ever
do some jive
somersaults in cannon
ball games where Mays uses basket
catches to improvise proverbs of
what did I do
to be so black and blue
skylines in my mother's
folded prayers

Or did her ever
wear polka
striped laughter with Monk ad
libbing where-a
bouts of the Champ floating
like a butter
fly and stinging like a be
bopping tenor wasp

I music who wears
music war
robes of definitions
where the great white
wash
board of directors
do
not possess telescopes
to peep at the next
minute

Best
feeling I ever had
I fell off the clif
ford brown sedan
with half muted
mufflers and hydraulic
lips to syncopate poison and sweet
potatoes for tomorrow's day
breaks into violent scats
with Jug

XVIII. Eighteen

I can hitch
hike my way to heaven with
out the what's goin
on in Marvin's pleas

and I finally
get a taxi Cab
Calloway to Heideho
Heights where Tolson
opens a gallery
in his Harlem night
train

where he wears khaki
gloves for his spirit

Midnight
is a bridge across
miles of kinda blue
brothels of interrogators
crying some day my prince
will come down
from his high C to loop

the loop with Wilson
or any picket fence
accepting stolen lyrics
on credit

I turn
the fun of a lonely guitar
man into long road
maps of rhythmic decades
I riff on week
end tables where my solos

are moats a
round orphaned prayers

aquatic
                blues riffed up
side downtown on corners of
vacant lots of concern

I give

For my song
battles eugenic accidents of hours
with genetic cries
I inherit

My
music collects old calendars
empires and assassins and
moses and exoduses and prophets
and golden dusted names
folded in yellowed obituaries
of silences and time

I take
inventions of languages and
I invent
I invent

events of clouds and brick
masons and Niles and rhythmic
testimonies of thieves
bidding for my name

Killer Joe and Stagger
Lee in denim neck
ties at the Trianon

Tattered rims of lynch
ropes and Small's Paradise

Old calendars of wars
my music collects

I decide
on my journey
where my soul been anchored
in the chords

In the chords
In the chords
In the chords

My soul
been anchored in the chords

XIX. Birth of any Chaos

From Von
I learn all
ways to be
bopping voyages into ball
ads on windows of absence
where I
review history

When I
sit at the fire
place hear
say is the back
log of my conversation
with spaces between
silences in my sorrows

But here
my axe screams
so loud I hurt my finger
prints as it hitch
hikes to heaven and back
seats of mercy
I ride

All
ways I throw my voice
a bone
                because it displays

architectural flower
pots and pan
cakes on menus of
my dreams

From Von
I learn the birth of any chaos
is the embryo of my poem's
quest for a language
not yet rooted in silences

I learn
from Von because I can see
his fingers maneuver nuances
from Mars or Venus or corner
gossip from some
where in the universe

with riffs of a predator
devouring anthems of its victim's
wails for breath out there night after
night in the New Apartment Galaxy beyond

sound and silences an ax
man hacking paths across
part of God's creations riffing
and riffing and riffing his name
on a geography of wind

XX. MY SOUL'S GEOGRAPHY

From Be-Bop
I learn
the awkward step
is really a sophisticated ballet
pirouette of the mind

where one perceives
the choreography only

after its broken
limbs are dissected   for humpty
dumpty is the Rosetta Stone of
art   the multiplicity of fragments

battered against distances
brings the song from their innards

I long
the challenge of retrieving
my songs from death's pulverizing hand
shakes with my flesh   may the lobotomy of
my trek into silence be a long
song

For I
witness and witness but tell
no testimony Except
surveys I make of my soul's
geography

Humpty
Dumpty is a prophet of a time with
out calendars I

applaud him after
his fall   because I can
see more than ten axes

searching for his parts
to play them

My
songs never got chain
prints on their epics

All
ways got wings
on their hands

When
I got something to say I pay Humpty
Dumpty galactic tolls across distances
I do
not dream

I
consolidate families of bereaved
dreams when I
talk to Humpty
Dumpty

My
tale is penniless
only the ground volunteers
itself as a bed
ridden by a jockey
in stretch runs of pain

World
is Humpty Dumpty
and I
knock on its shelf
life put it back to
gathering my names a
gain

World
is Humpty Dumpty

It's all
right to say blues
to Jesus

It's all
right all
right

XXI. Blues Inside His Breathing

The
birth of chaos
is the embryo of my songs

voices I collect bits of nights
crushed by blind winds

I am
The
Old Man And the Sea
shore trying
to find images of a home
land in Otis
Redding's horizons

I hear some
body say they
hear some
body say Trane
say he takes blues out of the cold

brings it in
side his breathing

makes them lungs
of his music his invasions
into out
reach programs of chordal genius

he sponsors in tenor wonder land
scapes of the spirit chromatic greeting
cards he shuffles on
to soprano memoirs of vacant
skies

Where
I unbend circles
for Mall E
able roads

I know it is all
ways the ancient In/ca
barets of my dreams where lush life
is the official ballad of my soul

that blooms
bursting out of Jim
Crow's narrowing cells of get
back   get back   get back

If you drink white
lightning you all
right all right

How I
talk is a nation's speech
therapist in crises
where the unbridled universe
is my pony
express rider of breath

How
I play

takes a drunken accordion
and my axe gets black cat
scans for epilepsy because
the doctor can
not hear its voice sequences
vote for melodic epochs
in its head

One booga
loo and two spanks
equal three square
dances and I still
can add a moon
walk after one buck
and a wing

Where
blues is my mother
tongue lashes against
silences when my blood
strolls to meet whips
or chains or bullet
targets it is my mother
lung breathing languages
I inhale

I am an actor
with a bit part
in the hair of eternity
Anthony Quinn's shadow
challenges Charleston
Heston's Moses in a game of
stiff left
jabbs that take weeks
to extend beyond
their anemic grunts

Satchel hurls dead

drops on the out
side corner
stones of black identity near
Handy's legacy

where few alien objects
done invaded America's white
planetary desires for human
existence but Dizzy all

ways telling
his truth say Bird
mummifies his sound
do
not want his songs
appear naked in heaven

and when I
ask what if his music did
not make it
to heaven   Dizzy
say Be-Bop   speech God tosses
with His left hand
cuffs and I do
not believe His right
hand is for language

Did
you know that music in Indian
films kills more Indians
than small
pox or Custer

like Aboriginal musical
executions Indian music
in films sings Indians
to death
sentences in consciousness

I play
Whitman and lilacs
in his spirit and
I play
Billie and gardenias
in her high
ways' high
five affirmations of life
times in Babylon

Because   the road I travel
                    the road I travel
                    the road I travel

mighty long
mighty song

Dizzy all
ways say a poem
just your Bird
in flight with
a bite   says Von
stays in his hood
doing Be-Bop good

Says
No ship brings my music
in chains No auction
block names it   No slavery makes it pick
cotton or diddley
bo   This bit of earth
quake I wake
for my Vitamin D
natural blues

This Vitamin D
natural blues I get because
Sarah is Divine   a tragedian
Hamlet   a disciple of hers
wears his royal seal
of laughter inside or Little
Boy Blue dresses in solitudes of
Monk's Dream or the Sophisticated

Lady Duke plays
and Ella scats this
little light of mine

eyes done seen
the glory of the coming of
the chords

Coming of the chords
Coming of the chords
Coming of the chords

XXII. STILL BORN SONG

My
task is to solve my voice's finger
tips' extensions
for its daily languages
Where blues
is the negotiator of my songs

My
diurnal moans
are survival kit
carsons exploring new
territory my voice finds
in Bessie Smith's pig
foot and empty
bed again and again

Remember
there are no speed
limits in linguistic
voyages for self
expression of selves
lost no walkie
talkies surveying hiding
places for patrolmen with radar
guns aimed at pocket
billiards of your imagination

I come here
bound in chain
linked hostility

but weaving

language over avenues
of a thousand years
my memory has taught
seasons the geography of absent foot
steps

All
my life I have
had border war
zones with authority

Because
I am a power
forward pass in celestial
discourses with authority
where Jerry Rice argues
for slants over middle
of the road potions

And Karl
Marx drives in
side Lois
Lanes with his left
hand finger
roll mastery over part
time lies the master
advertises as obedience

Nameless
I sit naming names of nights
in their dark ward
robes of mystery in
side Hawkins' body and
soul man I am a soul
man Hawkins   The Midnight Tenor Man
Blues Sage hawking   pains on boulevards of melodious
journeys through windows
of the soul Where the Middle Passage
rests in some black mother's prayers
for delivery of her brown paper
bag of dry
bones with her still
born song's name in it   No
body knows the troubles
I see coming down yonder's wall

The Auction Block
club was
not about civic pride or neighbor
hood improvement   It was a gossip
column of marching thieves
My
ballads some
times sweep and clean house
boy's ears for it   And Some
times I feel like a mother
less child cooked for it

XXIII. Knowing The Hand That Hoes

In my hours I cultivate
where South
Africa is a battle
field hand and
America is a plantation
owner

Archipelagos of tomorrows
pulverized in chaos
I survey
with tenor care
packages of ballads

When
Trane was winning
cases he had Elvin assisted
by Lloyd in the back court
marshals

Blues
lyrics are emergency
numbers to heaven

stretched

from Mississippi
to the next star
ships waiting for white

to tell some

of my people

its all
right all right
to think all
right all
right

Blues
the SOS of the universe

The city
is Humpty Dumpty's
utopia where he falls and
falls and falls

I
come out of nothingness

out of chaos
I come
with my wealth
on my lips

In my land
there are more cattle
bred than any bull
shit can impregnate
with the milk
of human kindness
where my axe
keeps its ear
to the ground
hog's shadow

Every
morning I rise
with wasp sting
ray guns on automatic
pilot licenses of Adam
Smith and Eve
Arden

My
axe got the chromo
somes of disorder
and sings wreck
ages of dissolution

where I know heroes
by the terminals of
languages they leave me
to survey
as my own sound
on the long hard
drive ways of caprice

Thunder
celebrates its anniversaries
in my axe's memory
because I get my salvation
army fatigues
for a buck and
a quarter of a smile

I am music I make
I am wind I breathe
I am space between spaces I find
I am a whole in fragments I pattern
I am a voice in voices I construct
I am ways into myself

I am the road
maps of my journey
when my axe sings

It is a well
kept mood
indigo secret

     jazz

repairs Humpty Dumpty's soul
train's danger box
cars of rhythms with right cross
over melodies and left hook
worms eating debris
so the alley's cats
can find Ella or Sarah
or Betty Carter

Any
time I find breakages
like I get keys to in
side ball
bearings annoying my spirit
with steel jabs
moving like Ali
Baba's legends

Beyond
my axe's voyages all
ways there is life
I search for

I play
story lines
of march of
dimes and
diamond mines at Kimberley's
ancient hole where martyr's
skeletons' fill empty
space where dreams once spoke SeSotho
enchanted nights of owner
ships sailing in lineage
names Or cotton

fields in Mississippi
with ebony skin sweating
lyrics Robert Johnson
teaches his guitar on midnights
after they tar and
feather dreams of his days

The burden of knowing
the hand that hoes
my dreams for its daily
blood I play

XXIV. Night Epics

Wilkerson climbs up
on the roof red
topping after
hours The Last Drifter
in a millennium to abuse
an axe while the Bowie

nights cut a whole deck with trump
edible riffs with rib
tip passes from Magic behind the back
door man trying to stop
Michael from rising high
as the highest C in his solos Bowie
nights in Middle Passage dreams

whispering nuances whispering muted
echoes of Shango and Ogun repealing
authority of Auction Blocks and whip
lashes against memory Bowie
nights long epics coiled in Lester's
aisles of new beginnings

I begin
each day in another galactic
tenor moment with Bird and the yard
bird dog his riffs sick
on stagnant waters in the wind's
tears   going some

where from ain't no
body's business if I do
not buck
dance for the shadows
who own club

houses where I play or if I do
not buck
and wing dang doodle on the skin of air
as I journey one more mile
for a melody I am beginning
to know

One more mile
One more mile
One more mile

Oh, Lord
my axe gotta go
after it has gone its journey
long riffs behind dirges

where jive takes death's foot
prints from dust
calls o limb
o limb o limb
o limb o limb
o rise while I cast a
net for your dances

One more mile

XXV. TWENTY-FIVE

I have this special
place I create in a pit
bull's mouth
full of danger
zones thirty two
or more to be exact

where I risk every
thing because I long Humpty
Dumpty's freedom yet I believe

in fertility of absences
therefore yesterday
is a delta
where I plant voices
I long

Though
he is male Bird
is my mother
wit that unscrambles Humpty
Dumpty's flesh tones

The
hole in my mother's dough
nut 'em egg
rolls is a vestibule
to ABCs of my morality

I was twelve and Bo
Diddely was no older
when a Chess Record shop
lifter picked his soul
for a signed
contract and I never for

get the game
warden of creativity looking
the other way
ward glances
at me too

I am a small axe
and I cut down big
trios   drum bass
and pianisiamos of a key
boarder in my silences

In my voyages
from my battle
ship mate Bird I strike the queen bee
bopper Ella as she scats wop speed
ometers for Jimi's fingers
pointing new hosannas from down
homes blues tributaries over
flowing into Chicago or Kansas
City or Memphis or St. Louis
Woman with Caldonia's head
rag

I strike
imaginations in my journey
from Ife fossils where I be Da
homey grooves of rap
black, beige, and brown

stones in Bed Sty
where axmen remember roots
in Kunta's eyes

I strike
imaginations where my axe
travels to its voice's boundaries

and boundless invitations
to seek its voices

XXVI. Twenty-six

When
I solo I am a Bird soaring
I am Dizzy
I catch the Trane
I pack up my Bags
I journey Miles
Till I reach a Monk
Get myself a Jug
Then drink Muddy Waters
Have lunch with a Duke
Jive with a Count
And write the Prez
Get baptized by Newk
On Green
Onion Avenue where I
get my pickles and good
foots from Poppa's
brand new bag

dad who won't pay child
hood allegiances or memory
support for his five
long years with Short
Fat Fannie and the dancing
in the street
cars of Harlem on my mind

I like a hot Jelly Roll
that makes me rag
time rag
distance rag
day rag any
thing I rag
time till my
axe learns that it can
not put things back to
gathering again
but it can

conjure Humpty Dumpty's
bits into pulses of
breathing into dances

Dizzy says no
body got much talons
in their voice
as Lady Day
light saving
time she got so much
its tears gardenias
from her tone

and her song bleeds
silence and distances in
side her lungs
that limp because of
their mighty heavy
lodes

The Lady's song
chilly water
moccassin spreading its skin with
the venom its sucks
from pains in some poor
girl's   heart
aches   good morning
blues   blues how do
you do I am feel all
right but blues how
is you chilly water
moccassin with
out venom spreading
skin to suck away pains

My
axe is Moses' staff and
Franklin's lightning
rod and reel

I use
to fish
for bits of Humpty Dumpty's week
end games I play
during an exodus
from a third floor with a one
way out
rageous circumstance
where I be
bopped a
way from her man down
stairs with a freindly smile
and a stoic forty
five gritting its trigger with

out Roy Rogers to who
a him who
a who a him who
a him

XXVII. SOLO

When
my axe fails to sing morning
glories or roses
I sick
my canon ball
point pen on you

in his land
where the governmental
word is as memorable
as the life
expectancy of a bad
joke

I am many tongues
because jazz language
layered and layered
on into infinity

permission to seek
identity on personal
bases without being
picked off by Gibson or
Marichal

A convert to Catholicism
without a sword demanding
my neck

I am a stand up
comedian on strike
missions over a papal bull
goring my humanity
with its Asiento horns
I do
not have qualms with the God with
out walls of my instructions

My
knees rehearse
genuflections to Him

who leads me toward
language galactic leaps
to explore exits from door
ways   For God is saying
I am from chaos   Humpty Dumpty
is a prophet of mine
because limitations you get
rid of are the domain markers
on in
to in
finite foot
steps of voyagers seeking language
they speak

When I am
free of language I find
I compose out of nothingness
I own if chaos were nickles
and dimes I would put billion
air
wind bags to shame
with my wealth

When
my grand
mother wanted to teach
she would
move her hands
like she sewing
or knitting
but there would be no
thing but water streaming
down her hands on
to her apron in her lap

then she would
say I am plaiting hair of a
cloud that bring this summer
shower yesterday I find two pieces of wind
I gonna wash put in basket
for my next quilt

Language is a bridge across
chasms speech is afraid
to negotiate It is the measured
voice of measureless distance
and time

When
I solo I play
it some
times I feel like a motherless child
hood

I play
holes of dough
nuts for my axe's desert sweet
water
melons on vines of trombones
climbing lazily
to introduce fingers
to lyrics its voice inters
in meadows of brass
knuckles its tone whisper
to depths of liquidity's
mausoleum

When I
get to the air
port of authority
before I blow I

check my satch
mo better blues

XXVIII. History, Hollers, and Horn

All
the voices in the universe
I contact I

speak

when
I solo on voyages in
to selves in
side my
self I need
to explore

My
axe is not the Enola Gay
so it does
not huff or
puff away places

It
seizes with eyes piercing
skin of clouds
or moral codes   It does
not invite light of a thousand light
years at its front door
way to where black
rain falls like Dinah's
blues on this bit of earth
quakes

I
belong to a land of
a thousand dances

and
my axe is not the Enola Gay
chaps or gals at the bar
be cued shadow of a hundred
thousand or more

at Hiroshima or
Nagasaki where language
failed to enchant veins
with songs

All
ways I travel knowing
the language I seek is with
in a universe in
side me where
on the day I was born
I
knew I would never know
the entire history of my horn

Spirituals and toasts
and field
hollers and blues
and sermons and
swing and Dixie
land and be
bop are stops on the road
I travel

where I know
I will never know
the entire geography of
my horn

But I
will come out
each night and I will solo

and travel where
ever my horn leads me
on let me stand

December 12, 1996

Sterling D. Plumpp

.